THE MENTALITY OF PREACHING:
THE THREE-QUESTION METHOD

DR. ANTIONE J. HUTCHINS, SR.

COPYRIGHT

<u>**JOURNAL JOY**</u>

An *Imprint* of Journal Joy *Publishers*

www.thejournaljoy.com

DEDICATION

I dedicate this book to the two people who were there when it all began, my parents. My father went on to be with the Lord about a year before this book was finished. His legacy is left in his children, and this book is a result of the fruit of his labor in life. My mother is one of the strongest women I know. When I look at the many things in life that she has endured, I am encouraged to never stop going. Life is an unpredictable roller coaster ride. I am grateful to God that He has allowed me to see what tenacity, resilience, and perseverance look like by watching my mom and dad over the years of my life.

CONTENTS

FOREWORD

by Dr. Charles E. Goodman, Jr.

"For since, in the wisdom of God, the world knew not God, it pleased God by the foolishness of preaching to save them that believe"

1 Corinthians 1:21 NKJ

Since I was a little boy, I have always been enamored with preaching. Watching the men and women who I saw grace the pulpit with eloquence and power in the small holiness church I grew up in intrigued me. I saw preachers take the Word of God to explain, correct, lead and deliver. I witnessed a range of sermons, from well-organized and thoughtful to disjointed and passionate sermons. I have seen sermons build up, and I have also seen sermons tear down. Throughout my spiritual formation, the sermonic moment has always been centered in my worship experience and relationship to God. No matter the shape, form, and style of the sermon preached, I experienced first-hand, how the preaching compelled people to respond with a desire and sole intent to be saved in a relationship with Jesus. I was instantly hooked, and just could not get enough of the preached word.

This great fascination led me to accept my own call in preaching and pastoral ministry. I have dedicated my life to being a student and practitioner of preaching. Not only am I captivated with the substance and style of preaching, I also am equally engaged with the preparation and insight of the preacher. Preaching cannot be separated from the person, passion and collective experience of the preacher. For this reason, not only do I study and personally benefit from the different types of preaching such as expository, narrative, topical, etc., but I listen to the great men and women who have a unique and canny ability to make the "book talk".

Preaching and sermon development is hard work. Being someone who has to do it multiple times weekly, I know the strain and stress of preparation and performance. Figuring out how to approach the text with integrity and insight, through the lens and tools they teach in seminary, is difficult and rewarding work. Whether it's finding the tension of the text, accurately exposing the author's meaning of the text and then explaining the ancient text in a way that is understandable for a contemporary audience. Exegesis is hard and tedious work. The old adage is true, "Sermons don't grow on trees". We as preachers are always in search of new, fresh and innovative approaches to preparing and preaching that maintain the integrity of faithful scriptural study and powerful and applicable preaching that reaches people where they are with the truth of God's word.

This book, "The Mentality of Preaching: The Three Question Method" by Dr. Antoine Hutchins is a ground breaking and kingdom shaking resource for any preacher that wants a fresh, innovative and applicable way to approach preparing and preaching impactful biblical sermons. It is a literal game changer in the approach and field of homiletics.

I met Dr Hutchins some years ago and God has knitted our lives and ministries together in a way that can only be explained through covenant relationship. Not only is Dr Hutchins a preacher, but a pastor as well, who week in and week out, goes about the business of preaching to a local congregation and beyond. I say with no hesitation nor trepidation, he is the best preacher I know. A unicorn and one of one, with a gift set that defies convention, Dr Hutchins takes sermonizing seriously and presents it in a clear and powerful way.

When I first heard Dr Hutchins incorporate his 3 question method into public proclamation, I was floored and amazed. It's simple and straightforward. It covers the summary of the sermon, background of the text, sermonic tension and resolution of the chosen text, and places it in a digestible form that all who listen can grasp it, understand it and apply it.

It gives the preacher a new way of comprehending the text and preaching from preparation overflow that allows the preacher the freedom and fluidity to share sermonically by seamlessly connecting the sacred desk in the study and the sacred desk in the sanctuary. The study and practice of homiletics will officially no longer be the same!

This book that is in your hands, will help build your foundation/confidence in formulating sermons that will not only allow you to be your authentic self, but also connect with the congregation in an impactful and poignant way. It is a step by step manual to help you apply this 3 question model to your own study and delivery, which can easily be incorporated in your own style. Watch how your effectiveness as a communicator and preacher exponentially increases. Be prepared to be challenged, stretched and transformed in your preaching. I know I have.

In Awe of God's Grace in Preaching, I remain,

Dr. Charles E. Goodman, Jr.

Senior Pastor/Teacher

Tabernacle Baptist Church

Augusta, GA

Introduction

What is the mentality of preaching? What questions need to be answered in order to deliver an impactful sermon? Are you aspiring to be successful in a specific area of ministry? If you're interested in the answers to these essential questions as a preacher of the Gospel, then this book is for you. I've learned that the mentality of preaching encompasses church administration, church revitalization, preaching, and teaching. It's also important to note that the key to ministry as a whole is not being a superstar but constantly striving to have an all-star team, or what I call a "Dream Team." This book is a testament to my ministry of making other disciples. The goal of this book is to make you feel comfortable with yourself in terms of how you approach ministry, and especially how you approach preaching.

When it comes to the preaching aspect, this Three-Question Method came out of a season of me having to shift from an old method of preaching that just was not working for me. I had to come up with a different approach, which caused me to stretch myself. This behavioral modification approach, which is outside of tradition, will most likely stretch you also. I've found that this approach is not just a good idea, but a *God* idea, and that the weight of your sermon is measured by what's left on the floor.

In chapter 1, I discuss how we got here, the context behind the creation of the method. I propose that preaching can be clear, relevant, and impactful without negating the element of time management. I address the realities that there was a need for better time management and that preaching is a part of church revitalization.

In chapter 2, I highlight the biblical basis and framework for different preaching styles. I propose that the person that you are must give yourself permission and exposure to evolve into who you are going to be. I expound on reasons why it's okay to be different, the theology of the method, and personal preaching influences.

In chapter 3, I provide license for the preacher to be authentic to themselves. I propose that influence versus imitation are two different approaches to being the effective you that God has called. I provide exposition on Phillip Brooke's quote, "Preaching is truth through personality" (Lyman Beecher Lectures at Yale).

In chapter 4, I get into the actual Three-Question Method itself. I expound on how question one leads into question two, which gives a platform for question three.

I hope to give you some tools to better understand the mentality of preaching and learn a nontraditional approach to sermon development and delivery, all while being authentically you, to the glory of Almighty God.

CHAPTER 1
HOW WE GOT HERE

Time Management

When one is serious about preaching the Gospel, that seriousness presents the challenge of constantly having more messages than you have time. The natural instinct of a zealous preacher is to get everything that is inside of them out to the listening audience, almost to the point of spiritual force-feeding. Extension of preaching time does not necessarily equate to an increase of impact for the hearer. Preaching can be clear, relevant, and impactful without negating the element of time management.

The Three-Question Method was divinely inspired… as an accident, actually. I say that because I did not know I was going to come up with a method. I did not foresee that this formula for preaching was going to be so impactful to listeners, and more so appealing to other preachers. I literally did not realize that the method was going to go beyond the church that I pastored.

Church Revitalization

The evolution of a customized sermonic formula was born out of the frustration of a senior pastor who is intrigued with the aspects of church revitalization. My definition of church revitalization is the maximizing of potential for a congregation, regardless of size, to have the greatest impact, within their capacity, for the Kingdom of God. This maximization takes place through the collaboration of what I like to call the three foundational Ps of church revitalization. The three foundational Ps that I consider vital to church revitalization are biblical principles, a spiritual posture, and administrative processes. Synergy between all three, the principles, the posture, and the processes, is necessary if the congregation is to experience true church revitalization.

In order to understand the need for the preaching method, one must be aware of where preaching fits with regards to church growth. In my near thirty years of ministry experience, I have become aware of four basic elements needed for church growth. These four foundational corners of church growth are:

1. Sound biblical preaching/teaching

2. Attractive music

3. Parking

4. Time management

Sound biblical preaching/teaching is priority. Anything done in the pursuit of revitalizing a congregation cannot be accomplished with mere great ideas. The steps taken to revitalize a church must be biblically based. A congregation should always be able to point the practices of their church back to the bible in some way, shape, or form. John 1:1 is clear that, "In the beginning was the Word..." This first part of that scripture should encourage congregations to begin with the Word of God. Biblical basis is the key foundational element in church revitalization.

The second element required for church growth is attractive music. In 1 Samuel 16:14–23, King Saul is plagued with an evil spirit. The only relief that he can find is the skillful playing of young

David on his harp. Music ministry is what drives the evil spirit away so that King Saul can regain and maintain his clarity of thought. If this biblical principle teaches nothing else, it shows that when people are properly ministered to musically, the preacher can then preach to clear-minded listeners.

Parking is the third component of church revitalization—and one of the most underrated . This component is a major issue if a congregation is going to be successful at church growth. No matter how much people enjoy the worship experience, after a short period of time, many get frustrated and turned off by the repeated inconvenience of getting in and out of worship services, ministry events, and meetings.

The fourth basic element of church revitalization is time management. In the fast-paced culture of the day, people are more calendar-driven in their everyday routines. Monopolizing congregants' time is only going to get a church but so far. Worship can be structured in a way that allows for an impactful experience while eliminating fillers in the program that are redundant and purposeless outside of ego gratification of the pulpit and/or the pew.

One of the challenges in the collaboration between biblical preaching and administrative processes is the tension of the two elements of preaching and process when dealing with the issue of time management. At the time of embarking upon church revitalization within our congregation, the issue of time management in the worship services was being made more difficult due to how long the preaching was. To put it plainly, I was preaching too long.

At a certain juncture of the church experiencing revitalization momentum, we had no choice but to go to multiple services. Within the time structure of our multiple services, if we did not get out at a certain time (time management), then the congregants getting in and out of worship had parking issues. Simply put, we had a weekly traffic jam and parking lot tension. The only way to efficiently serve everyone when it came to worship each week was to develop a regimented time schedule.

No, we were not limiting the move of the Holy Spirit. We were limiting the people who were hijacking worship services through unnecessary rhetorical activity. So, if you were the worship leader, or had any role on the platform, the staff strategized a certain amount of time to serve in that particular capacity. The worship designers would inform participants: "This is your slot. Now, when we give you that slot, we're not limiting your anointing. We're limiting how much time you want to take up, because God doesn't need a warmup—you do."

This intentionality of planning would provoke those who were participating to show up fully prepared. If the worship leader was given six minutes to do the call to worship, the opening prayer, and read the scripture, being prepared caused those six minutes to be extremely impactful and set the pace for others coming behind them. If the worship leader was constantly unprepared, it exposed the lack of discipline in that individual that perhaps needed to be further developed through training and mentorship.

One being consistently unprepared for assignments that were given in advance is not God's fault, nor is it an indictment on the movement of the Holy Spirit. Yes, the staff of the church would hear the complaints from those who didn't see a need for discipline while serving on the platform—things such as, "Come on, now. You all are stifling the move of the Holy Spirit." Since we were dealing with leaders who should see the need to be an example in leading, the private response in meetings would be, "No, we are not stifling the move of the Holy Spirit. The Holy Spirit was already here and ready to go when we showed up. We are merely putting you in a place of accountability and discipline. As leaders, this stretches all of us to be more effective in ways that challenge and grow us." Of course, that posture was not readily accepted at first. However, the more the staff saw the process work, the more everyone jumped on board.

When one has a committed personal relationship with God and a devotional life, that individual constantly seeks to live in the presence of God. Under those conditions of constantly seeking to be in God's presence, those individuals leading worship are inviting people into an atmosphere that they already live in daily. At that point, one can literally get up and do their assignment in the time slot allowed. This readiness should be the momentum-provoking moment needed for the person coming behind them on the platform.

With all of that being stated, I, as a leader, never want to give people assignments that I am not willing to adhere to. In order to exemplify that operating in discipline with effectiveness can be done, we, as the strategizing team, placed my preaching slot on a timetable as well.

I fully understand the norms that we as preachers operate in from behind the pulpit. Most of us feel as if we have something so uniquely important to say that we should take as long as we want to say it, all in one setting. This practice of long-windedness is what could be considered as spiritual force-feeding each week. You will win the battle of preaching the whole bible in one sermon, but you may lose the war. People will eventually start to pick and choose when they come back.

Yes, you may even have a week here and there where the response of the congregation will push you to keep being undisciplined. This inconsistency is not recommended because people don't respond to great moments as much as they respond to consistency. Most people, given a choice, even in worship, would rather have an average experience consistently than a great experience every now and then. In my experience, there is a sense that congregants adhere better to managed expectations. When people are conditioned to what they will get on a regular basis, those people position their expectations accordingly. The Holy Spirit, within the worship experience, then has an opportunity to operate according to Ephesians 3:20, "Now unto him that is able to do exceeding abundantly above all that we ask or think, according to the power that worketh in us."

When I put myself on the time clock, I gave twenty-five minutes of sermon time at the early service and thirty-five minutes of preaching time at the main service. Mind you, this holding of accountability using the countdown clock is totally contextual. I'm not suggesting that you minimize your preaching slots to those time frames; I am simply informing you of what our church had to manage and maneuver at the time. Our staff and I came up with those slots just to stay on a realistic time schedule. We did not want the early service to have the perception that they were being slighted, nor did we want the main service to feel as if we just dragged their worship experience out as long as possible, since it was the final worship service of the day.

As a result, every participant in the worship experience would be on a regimen. The main worship service was larger in attendance, so it took a little more time to facilitate. This added time of facilitation is why there were thirty-five minutes on the clock for that worship service as opposed to the twenty-five minutes for the earlier service. The challenge was that even the thirty-five minutes were antithetical to the style of preaching that I had done my entire career. With fifteen minutes left on the clock, I was just coming out of the explanation of context before giving a relevant question, let alone the answers to the question. I had not even gotten into my first point before I found myself rushing and having to end the sermon early for the sake of discipline. I was frustrated, aggravated, and discouraged each week, feeling as if I was missing the opportunity to be more effective.

When I started my classes in the doctoral program, one of the professors told us, "The weight of a sermon is measured by the pieces that get left on the floor." Oftentimes, the reason that the sermon is so long is because we don't want to leave any pieces on the floor. But as a pastor, what I had to come to understand is: You preach every week. Use those pieces next week, or put them in a series, or put them in the pocket for when you come back around somewhere near that subject or that text again.

That clock was kind of beating me, especially during the early services. Furthermore, if I'm harping on time management, I have to be the first partaker of the fruit. So, I would cut out the intro, and just jump right into the text. Still wasn't enough. I would try to just do two points instead of three, and it just wasn't working. I was prepared each week when I stood up to preach. I would sometimes even wonder if I was too prepared, if there is even such a thing. I was determined that there had to be another way.

The Revelation and the Shift

James 1:5 says, "If you need wisdom, ask our generous God, and He will give it to you. He will not rebuke you for asking." In frustration, more intense prayer began to play a factor during my study time. That intense prayer is what I believe birthed a homiletic revelation. This revelation would change how my sermon would be delivered going forward. The revelation would be later called the "Three-Question Method."

Normally in my studies, a propositional statement, also called a thesis statement, would be crafted after resource exploration. This propositional statement, as taught in the seminary I was privileged to attend, would be the central theme of the sermon and the beginning of sermon construction. The introduction, context explanation, relevant question, and answers to the question, as well as the celebration in closing the sermon, would revolve around this propositional statement.

The first part of the homiletic transition was developing the propositional statement into the actual entire introduction. This statement would shift from a singular purpose of being the central theme to becoming the introduction of the sermon, leading with the sentiment, "If I had to sum this sermon up into a single sentence, I would simply say…" At this point of the declaration, the propositional statement would then be plugged into the sentence in order to complete the introduction. Yes, this one statement became the entire introduction and saved a lot of time. The statement was concise and explained the very takeaway that the sermon was attempting to convey from the sermon's inception. We will dig into the details of the propositional statement formation further down in coming chapters. For now, let's continue with the overview.

One of the most effective ways to gather relevant information is to constantly ask questions of the biblical text. While looking at texts, reading commentaries, listening to other lectures, and reviewing whatever other resources are studied, I ask questions. My belief, since I was a young preacher, is that the difference between an impactful preacher and a noneffective preacher is their ability to ask questions in their study. The inquisitive preacher is the learned preacher; that preacher is going to do research in order to get the needed answers. These answers that have been developed during study would be the next part of my homiletic revelation.

The next part of the shift in sermon construction was using the answers to my questions, which were obtained through study, as the meat of the sermon itself. Again, we will get into the intricate details of this process in the coming chapters. This chapter is to merely explain how the process evolved. I would narrow the study questions down to the three most significant, based on the propositional statement. Though the propositional statement is the introduction, the statement must still stand as the central theme of the sermon.

This method was constructed out of the need for time management, but turned into something far more impactful than I could have imagined. This astounding breakthrough was a humanistic unintentional experiment that later proved to be a divinely inspired revelation given by the Holy Spirit. This revelation is what I earlier referred to as a divinely inspired accident that turned out to be no accident at all. Romans 8:28 reminds us that "All things work together for the good of them who love God, those who are the called according to His purpose." There are no accidents in the things of God, but rather things that work in harmony together for God's purpose.

This seemingly fragmented sermon, in comparison to the style of manuscript I had always written before, was what was being taken to the pulpit. Unsure how the new experimental structure would come across, I figured one Sunday would not cost the war should it not go well. In my mind, taking a propositional statement as an introduction and three questions that would be answered in a narrative way went against the formalities taught in seminary. My thought process at this point was not about using my seminary training the way it was taught to me. My mentality at this point was about making the greatest possible impact in a time-managed environment. I had no idea, nor any expectation, of whether or not this would work. To my surprise and relief, the feedback from the congregation after worship was overwhelmingly positive.

The Three-Question Method worked that first Sunday it was presented. Still a little skeptical, I said to myself, "Let me try it again next Sunday." The following week, I attempted to do the three questions again. The feedback was even more overwhelming. In my limited thinking, there was a new in-house way for me to feed the sheep the best sermonic food I was capable of in a managed amount of time. My three questions kept evolving over time. The more I asked questions, the more I realized I could control how long it took for me to answer the questions sermonically.

Finally, I started meeting my time schedule slot on the administrative timesheet. As I started to get more proficient at answering the questions, I was sometimes even giving a couple of minutes back. The feedback from the congregation was that people felt as if they had been in weekly Bible Study and Sunday Worship at the same time. The members began writing down the questions, along with the answers to the questions as they listened to the narrative answers. When we would get to the celebration of the sermon, people would be even more receptive due to the enlightenment they received, feeling as if they had been spiritually fed during the entire sermon without having their patience exhausted. Because the questions and answers were centered and fueled based on the propositional statement, the entire sermon stuck to the point and made sense to the hearers.

To be transparent and honest, although I was getting more and more comfortable with this newfound sermonic formula, I would only use it for the congregation where I pastored due to the threat of external scrutiny. When I went out on the road to preach for itinerant speaking engagements, I would go back to manuscripts and my familiar sermon structure. The problem for me was the lack of comfortability in using the old manuscript. The style in which I had preached for most of my career just wasn't the same feel. From an audience connectivity standpoint, my previous sermon structure, based on feedback and the engagement with the congregation, did not give the same level of impact. The shift in sermonic structure literally changed how I would now see preaching for the rest of my life. Preaching this new formula still, however, took some time to share sermonically with external congregations.

After about four months of using this new method, I accepted an outside engagement preaching at a large church in another part of the country. The church at the time had three morning worship services. The pastor that I was preaching for told me, "Hey, in our middle service… you don't have a lot of time. Just give your lesson and get out." I thought to myself, *Well, if I use this new Three-Question Method, it'll help me with the time aspect. If it doesn't work, the reputation is: That crowd is not the most responsive crowd. So, nobody will pay it any mind.* This was my first test run outside of the confines and comfort of being in my home pulpit. To my surprise, the preaching moment went amazingly well. The moment went so well that I went to the Three-Question Method for the rest of the day. I've rarely looked back since that day. This process of experiment by divine inspiration of the Holy Spirit is how I came up with this Three-Question Method.

Yeah, people don't understand that preaching can be clear, relevant, and impactful without negating the element of time management. Time management is not a bad word in a worship experience. Everything is time management. People now live by their clocks and their calendars. They literally plug in times for this, for that, for the other. The same way we feel about the respect people have for their time at work, their time at doctors' offices, their time at sorority or fraternity meetings—why not respect their time in worship as well?

So, as impactful as the other methods that I've used, studied, and learned in school are, I feel that this method is just as impactful and that it actually helps with the ability to control the time management aspect of preaching, especially when you preach on a weekly basis.

Having nearly twenty years of experience as a senior pastor and nearly thirty years of experience in ministry, I often tell starting pastors and young pastors that when it comes to leading a congregation, preaching is the steering wheel of a pastor's ship. Preaching is what turns the organization in directions that people need to look in. And if preaching is done effectively—and this is a church revitalization issue—it puts blinders on the congregation to only see what God wants them to see spiritually in that moment for them to walk towards. When a horse has blinders on, it's not a negative thing; it's not a bad thing. The blinders keep the horse from being distracted. The blinders keep the horse focused only on the direction that the driver needs the horse to go in. There's less conflict, there's less struggle with the horse, and there's less of a chance that the horse can be spooked by distractions and put everything else that is attached to the horse in jeopardy.

That's what preaching should do to a congregation. It should put blinders on. Not in a negative way, but in a positive way, to stay focused on the assignment that that congregation has. Whether it's in the community, whether it's spiritually, whether it's financially, whether it's project-wise. Preaching should put the blinders on so that you can just focus on whichever direction the ship needs to be turned in at that moment.

And that's a revitalization issue because if preaching isn't primary, the church won't be stable. Jesus says in Matthew 16:18, "Upon this rock, Peter, I'm going to build my church, and the gates of Hell shall not prevail against it." But what does he mean, "upon this rock"? It is not until Peter speaks and says what the truth is, "Thou art the Christ, the Son of the living God," that Jesus says, "And flesh and blood did not reveal this to you, but my Father, which is in heaven." And here's what I'll tell you upon this. I will say to you that thou art, Peter, *Petros* in Greek, means "a little pebble." And "upon this rock," in Greek, means "big boulder." So, he says, "With you hearing the truth, with you now..." Because faith comes by hearing, and hearing by the Word of God. "With you hearing and speaking the truth, flesh and blood did not reveal that to you. And that's what's going to grow you. That's what's going to expand you. And on that growth, on that expansion, I'm going to build my church, and the gates of hell shall not prevail against it."

This means the more you come into contact with knowing who God is, understanding who Jesus is, understanding what God has assigned to us in the earth for the kingdom of God, the more you grow and learn. Then, upon this rock, He'll build His church. Healthy things grow. The Word of God is what should be the primary medicine to keep the church of God healthy. And *that* is a revitalization issue.

It's okay to think through the process of the norm. Just because it's the norm doesn't mean it's the only way to do it. And what this method and this book should show us is that if you learn the norm, then you learn the parameters of how to do it a different way while still being correct.

Most of us are scared to step outside of what the norm is. We're scared of scrutiny; we're scared of being made fun of. We're scared that people are going to talk about us, and what originally had an intention of being innovative sometimes can end up being ... What's the word I want to use? *Mocked.* And most people are not willing to step outside of what the norm is in order to find a better way that fits them. We're going to talk about that in the next chapter, when it comes to doing things the way that fits the individual and not always limiting the individual to doing things the way everybody else does it.

C HAPTER 2

PERMISSION TO BE DIFFERENT

Why It's Okay to Be Different

As I stated in an earlier chapter, the Three-Question Method was never designed to go outside of the church that I pastored. It was only supposed to be a time management tool that helped me effectively deliver the Gospel. What happened was, the method leaked to the megachurch and to people who were watching outside of my congregation (because it was a megachurch, they had a lot of attention drawn to them). So, when preachers heard that there was a guest preacher, they wanted to watch. They heard the method, and people started asking questions. When I felt comfortable that the method would survive outside of the church that I pastored, I started using it while traveling during my preaching itinerary.

Eventually, it became a signature of my preaching. This signature is major for me and a lot, because if we rewind and back up to give further context, for most of my preaching career up until a few years before writing this book, I suffered from an inferiority complex. I always assumed that people were better at something and more knowledgeable at everything than I was, and that I was the low man on the totem pole.

I remember directing a choir in high school. We wanted to sing the song just like it was originally recorded. I heard a certain part and wanted to correct the way the sopranos were singing it and blending

19

with the altos. I stopped them and told them what I heard, and before we started over, everybody stood me down and told me that I was wrong. I immediately conceded because if everybody else stood me down, I did not want to be embarrassed. Of course, in my head, I was the low man on the totem pole, and they knew more than me. Obviously, they sang in churches and in groups outside of this high school choir in their individual contexts. Some of them were even background singers for professional artists, so I wasn't about to challenge any of them, only to discover down the road that all of them realized I was right.

I did not go back and give a gloating posture of me being right; I just tucked it in the pocket, kept on walking, and said, "Okay, a broken clock is right twice a day; maybe that was one of my two." Not realizing that I had a gift to hear, but did not trust the gift, I trusted other people. This is oftentimes the main handcuffing, shackling, oppressive, debilitating tool of the enemy in the midst of serving in ministry. The fear of criticism and being wrong makes us conform to the norm.

So, by the time I got to the point of developing this Three-Question Method, the reason it wouldn't leave my home pulpit was because I'm used to people doing things the way of the norm and I did not want to be the odd man out. I did not want to be talked about around the country. I thought, *If I just keep this to the people that I pastor because they love me and my preaching, they'll put up with me when everybody else will talk about me. Let me just use this on them*, not realizing my gift was making room for me.

Many times, people just need permission to be themselves, and because they don't have permission to be themselves, gifts are stifled, abilities are hindered, and personalities are suppressed because of fear of operating incorrectly and the possibility of public scrutiny.

It is the moment you get past people's opinions that God can truly use you. Phillip Brooks's definition of preaching, in a lecture delivered at Lyman Beecher Lectures at Yale, is "communication of truth through personality." If I can paraphrase or Hutchin-ize this, so to speak, what it tells us is that preaching is delivering truth through the individual personality of the preacher, which means I cannot be effective if I'm only trying to be like somebody else. My maximum effectiveness comes from being myself.

What this Three-Question Method does is give the preacher permission to be themselves. It gives you permission to give truth through personality because the person that you are must give yourself permission and exposure to evolve into who you're going to be. So, to answer your question, there's no way that I could know whether or not I'm doing it right, unless I've already studied the formal way of how to do it in the first place: going to school, learning the different methods in homiletics, learning the different ways that a sermon is generally constructed, learning the different nuances and the different terms that different styles of sermon construction take. Then, I learned which ones did not work for me.

Theology Of The Method

I love the information of the dialectic method in preaching. That method prompts the preacher to give the thesis, then the antithesis, followed by the synthesis. However, for my personality, the dialectic method doesn't necessarily work for me. I've used it. I think it was relatively impactful, but it was not comfortable enough for me to authentically use my personality and my different approach to preaching. It just did not work for me.

The correlation method calls for a proposition. That proposition is then adjusted to form a personal proposition before going into more of a transitional question. It is a simple method, but requires intentionality that turns the simple into more of a thought-provoking challenge. I enjoy this method because it turns the complex into more of an applicable delivery for the preacher.

The application method and I, we get along great. I enjoy the simplicity of it and often used it as the basis method for former sermon manuscripts. I used this method more regularly than the other two previously mentioned. The application method helped me to focus on the most complicated parts of sermon thoughts and to remain simplistic in my delivery.

I enjoy all of these methods. You have to understand these different methods that seminary and formal training give you; when you learn which ones work for you and which ones do not work for you, you can be yourself with ease. The difference between you and another person is that you are you and they are them. It is not for you to be them, and it's not for them to be you. It is okay to be different, and most people operate in anxiety when they feel like they're going to be the odd person out. You have to be okay with being different.

Paul talks about it in scriptures in Acts chapter 12. He says there are differences in administration. There are differences in gifts. There are differences in how we operate in the spirit. It's okay to be different. If I put five people in a kitchen and only give them the instruction, "Make me some spaghetti," it's going to take them longer to come up with the recipe than it is for them to implement it. Some only use turkey, some like sausage and pork and beef, some like vegan, some like angel hair pasta, some like regular spaghetti, some only use thin spaghetti, some want to use zucchini pasta. Some want to use a certain brand, some want to use the other brand, and some want to make it from scratch.

If you take five different people from different upbringings, from different exposure levels, from different processing systems in their own intellect, and just throw them in the kitchen and tell them to make spaghetti, their differences are going to be the biggest hindrance in coming up with the recipe. The good news is that if you send five different people to five different kitchens, you're going to get five different recipes of spaghetti, and all of them may be amazing. Even though you're different, it does not mean you're wrong. In preaching, it's okay to be different. Just because you're different doesn't mean you're wrong. Here is the gauge as to whether or not it's right or wrong: Is it accurate? Is it found in scripture? Is it true gospel? Is it proper? If it's accurate, it can be argued as to whether or not it's proper.

Well, the Three-Question Method actually has pieces of all of these different methods that I just mentioned: the dialectic method, the correlation method, even the application method. Just because the Three-Question Method is born from other methods that, from a time management perspective, did not work for me doesn't mean the methods simply don't work. They did not work *for me*, but there are certain parts in each method that work for me. I use those parts to make sure that I accurately have the information necessary in a sermon to properly deliver the Gospel.

So, yes, every religion has a piece of some other religion somewhere in it. You can be Catholic or Pentecostal; both of them are going to take communion. You could be Episcopalian or Methodist; both of them are going to have some form of music. Every religion has different pieces of the other. It's a matter of preference. That matter of preference comes out of you being okay with yourself enough to understand *This doesn't work for me, That doesn't work for me, This other thing may work for me.*

I'm okay with having some friends say that the Three-Question Method doesn't work for them. They've tried it. They say it doesn't work for their personalities because they're more narrative preachers in general, without as much structure and points. They're more narrative individuals, so they felt like the Three-Question Method did not work for them. However, I have other friends who use it so masterfully that I almost want to give them the credit for it—and I'm the one who taught it to them. So, it's okay to be different. It's a matter of differences. It's necessary to have exposure, and exposure is a preacher's best friend.

Personal Preaching Influences

Some of my personal preaching influences are very diverse in their presentations. I enjoy a Noel Jones-style preacher for his intellect and energy, combined in a sermon that grows you, excites you, and challenges you, versus the different style of a Joel Olsteen type, who is going to be more topical, less energetic, and more disciplined in their level of excitement, but who also challenges you to think about yourself in a way that should provoke you to want to be a better person.

Then, there are the traditional preachers, in a sense, who, even if their delivery may not be my preference, their mentality is so amazing that it makes you want to listen to them, whether they are great at simply talking or good at giving information. I am a proponent of sitting at the feet of wisdom.

Chapter 3

AUTHENTICITY OF THE PREACHER

Influence Versus Imitation

There is the constant tension of the preacher to be theologically correct and authentic at the same time. In the previous chapter, I hit on it a little bit, but let's dig a little deeper into it. Though I talked about it being okay to be different, I want to make it clear here that *just because it's okay to be different does not mean that it's okay to come up with a different version of you that is inauthentic in order to be innovative.*

Most people struggle with the fact that their differences put them outside of the norm in terms of current culture. The bigger struggle is wrestling with the question: Is your difference a good idea to try to attract an audience that you normally wouldn't attract because you bring something different than most people would bring, or is your difference authentically you? Many times, influence versus imitation are two different approaches to you being the effective you that God called you to be. Even though I said earlier that preaching is truth through personality, that personality has to be authentic in order for transparency to really be effective.

I don't know of any preacher who is good at what they do without the influence of some other great preacher. Being influenced is when you watch, or are mentored by, preachers, and certain things about them rub off on you, according to what works for your authenticity.

25

It is important to know that just because you are influenced by another preacher does not mean that what works for them will always work for you. Influence simply gives you permission to find your own path based on critiques; you are discipled and mentored by seasoned preachers who expose you to the direction in which God is trying to take you. This influence can happen while in close proximity to other preachers or when gleaning from them from afar.

There is nothing worse than when a preacher tries to be somebody else, pegging themselves as different, and everybody sitting in the pew can see right through them. Yes, it's okay to be different, as long as that difference is authentically *you*. You have to not just give yourself permission to be different; you have to make sure that those differences are *authentic*. Nobody wants to hear the imitation of their favorite preacher by one of their preacher's fans. Before you dive into this Three-Question Method, before you get into the nuances of the different parts of the sermon, before you decide whether or not this works for you or you like it, ask yourself a simple question: Who are you? Because if you're not going to be yourself, no method is going to work for you effectively.

Be Yourself

One of the biggest shifts to my ministry is when I became okay with me. Prior to that, I always had anxiety. The bigger the venue, the bigger the platform, the more I scared myself out of being myself, the more I tried to be who I thought the people wanted to hear, the more I wasn't comfortable with my style. I thought I was too country in my twang. I thought I was too ghetto in my approach. I thought I was less polished in how I articulated when I got excited. When I would go back and watch the tapes, I would always be embarrassed, not realizing that the more I was just myself, the more people wanted to hear me. I would lose future opportunities by trying to be who I thought they wanted to hear.

When I went through enough life challenges and hardship experiences, like a divorce, dealing with things like having to leave a church for the sake of sanity brought me to a culmination one day: I no longer cared what people thought about me. I was just going to get up and be myself. I had no clue that that was going to be the shift of my entire ministry. My ministry shifted the day I decided that I was going to be me and let the chips fall where they may. That's the moment more people wanted to hear me. People don't want to hear who you'd like to be. They want to hear who you *are*. As you develop in who you are, people will go along for the ride, as long as they see the authenticity of who you are at every stage.

Power To Preaching

Being Dr. Hutchins now humbly has an impact on my ministry. Sometimes, I forget I even have the doctorate until somebody calls me "Doctor." I'm not walking around with this nose-in-the-air mentality, like "I'm Dr. Hutchins." No, I'm me, and I just happened to have earned a doctorate degree along the way. That authenticity brings power to your preaching because you start to discover the parts of you that enhance the parts of your preaching. The preacher who is not willing to be authentic is the preacher who is not willing to be impactful.

Imitations do not last long. There is a quote in the book *Seven Habits of Highly Effective People* where the author, Stephen Covey, says, "Whenever you come up with an amazing, innovative idea that nobody else has come up with, the next thing you ought to do is come up with another idea because that one is going to be admired and imitated. Somebody's going to figure out a way to do it even better than you after they practice what you came up with, so you go find another idea because all your good ideas will be imitated. Imitation is the highest form of flattery. Yes, I can imitate the idea because that idea just happened to work for my personality."

When I'm authentic in imitating something that I see, but I figure out how to tailor it to my personality and make it authentically me, I may sing a song that somebody else wrote, but I'm going to sing it my way. People might even like it better my way than they did the original because every good idea is going to be immediately imitated and perfected. So, be okay with being you, knowing that you can be imitated, but never duplicated. There's a reason you're the only one with your fingerprint. There's a reason you're the only one with your dental record. There is a reason that you have to go and get your eyes checked—everybody doesn't have universal vision. Everybody has different levels of vision. There is a reason you're the only one with your DNA: When God created you, He planned for you to be *you* for the rest of your life.

Whenever you get to the place where you are not good enough for God to use, you are insulting the God who created you in the first place. It's as if to say, "He didn't know what He was doing, so let me be who He probably intended to make me in the first place." Authenticity of the preacher is crucial to the impact of their preaching. Most people, especially in the early years of preaching, watch preachers who impress them, who bless their lives, or who are great influencers. Then, instead of them using that influence to sharpen themselves—because the Bible is clear: iron sharpens iron—instead of them using that influence to build their level of exposure, instead of them using that influence to actually see a starting place to develop their mentality of preaching, they're too busy trying to *become* the influence. That imitation is going to be detrimental to ministry because God is not trying to use the you who you're trying to craft yourself to be based on somebody else. He's trying to use the you that He *made* you to be. Yes, you will evolve.

Yes, you will develop. Yes, you will enhance. Yes, you will grow, but the key is to *stay true to yourself* while you're evolving. While you're enhancing, stay true to yourself. While you're developing, stay true to yourself. While you're growing, grow into the you that He's destined you to be. That is crucial.

So, when you talk about this Three-Question Method, you have to ask yourself the question: Who are you? Because that is going to be the driving force in how God uses you to properly articulate the Gospel. It's not about us; it's about the Gospel. God wants to use us and our individual personalities in order to project and advance the Gospel.

Chapter 4

The Three-Question Method of Preaching

Central Theme

Whenever we look at constructing a sermon, there always have to be certain parts that stand in universal order. The same way that it takes many ingredients to bake a cake from scratch, it takes many components to construct an effective sermon. And no matter which method that you hold to, each one of them has one thing in common: A sermon has to have a central theme.

When we talk about the central theme of a sermon, this is what some people call the thesis statement. Others call it the propositional statement. Regardless of what you call it, the gist of it, the premise of it, has to remain the same. Here is the premise of that statement: It has to be the central theme of your sermon, and everything in your sermon can, at some point, tie back to that central theme.

If this theme is going to be impactful, then it has to be clear, concise, and literally the sum of all that will be said in the rest of the sermon. The central theme should be reduced to one singular sentence. This is what I like to call "the sermon in a sentence." You will know if this sentence is accurate if, after you read the scriptural text and quote the sermon in a sentence, everyone understands exactly what message the text is conveying.

If you cannot sum up your entire sermon within one sentence, then perhaps you are trying to tie multiple sermons into one central theme. Find a central theme, figure out how to condense it down to one sentence, and use that as the premise of your sermon for the duration of the presentation.

Once you construct that central theme and put it into sentence form, you have just completed the introduction to your sermon, which will take all of sixty seconds to deliver. Throughout the explanation of this method, I will give a non-biblical illustration as a reference just to make the point of the parts within the sermon.

Our non-scriptural reference that we will use as a basis for our spiritual or our theological argument will be one of my favorite fairytale stories, *Humpty Dumpty*. For example, the central theme has to be summed up at the beginning in order to give people a baseline as to where the sermon's going. The fable, fairytale story, or children's story, as we will reference it, goes something like this: Humpty Dumpty sat on a wall. Humpty Dumpty had a great fall. All the king's horses and all the king's men couldn't put Humpty back together again.

If we were to look at this as if it were a scripture, we must then figure out, *What is the central theme to this particular sermon that we would build on from the scripture?* In this case, the theme would be positioning. Where you are is central to everything that will follow within this story. So, in surmising the central theme, summing it up into a simple sentence that gives a thesis or proposition statement that we can use as an introduction may look like: "According to our reference text, be careful where you sit—it could cost you everything." Everything following that statement must, in some way, tie back into the central theme of positioning. So, once you have that central theme, you now have a clear path in how to go about referencing, researching, and even regurgitating the information that the sermon is supposed to produce. So, the first component you have to have is a central theme. What is the sermon talking about, and can you put that into a single sentence?

In order to help with the nuances of this method, allow me to first give an overview of each question. Once we see the entire picture, we can then go into the step-by-step components of constructing a sermon with this method.

Question 1: What is the context?

The context of the text is key. The context is the backdrop on which the text is written originally in scripture. It is looking behind the curtain of the text. The power of research confirms that the more the preacher knows, the more context they can give. You must determine: *What about your practical application makes your question real or relevant?* The process for composition is research, narrative, practical application, and questions and answers. The narrative presents your argument or the story that you are telling. You cannot properly tell the story if you do not research what is going on behind the scenes of the text.

Question 2: Where is the tension in the text?

The tension in the text is the part in the narrative that challenges, exposes, or conflicts us as human individuals. Finding the tension in the text humanizes the sermon, which makes the sermon relatable and relevant. You must identify what the challenge is for the hearer. The tension in the text exposes and challenges the excuses not to adhere to the principal idea of the sermon. Question 2 always deals with the tension within the text between us as humans now and those in the bible at the time of the text.

Question 3: What is the resolution of the text?

The resolution of the text is the prognosis of the sermon. Resolution within the text may not always be good, and it may not always be bad; however, it is always to be found in the text. The resolution must tie in with the title of the sermon. The question will dictate the title. Contextual creativity is essential to revealing the answer that is in the text. The preacher must consult the text deliberately, intentionally, and exclusively for the resolution of the text. Just like on the *Chopped* TV show, the ingredients must come from the basket.

The Celebration/Close

Many people like the celebration of the sermon. Just like the dialectic method, the celebration is at the answer to the third question. Instead of coming up with another separate celebration moment, your answer to the third question should build into your celebration, thus giving it the same connections to another method. This building to a close does not necessarily mean that everything in the sermon was positive. Building to a close simply means that the preacher must find hope, even in negativity, and convey this truth upon exiting the sermon.

Each question must be routed in practical application. Just like the application method has to tell us how the point applies to our lives, the answers to the questions must be biblical and practical. It does not go into the sermon if we cannot relate it to where people's lives are today in order for those hearers to apply the scripture to their everyday lives.

The Three-Question Method: Step-by-Step

All of the previously mentioned components make up the Three-Question Method, and each component piggybacks off of the previous component.

One of the challenges of preaching a well-researched sermon is that sometimes, people can get drowned in information that has nothing to do with their personal lives, where they are now, where they have been, or where they're going. All they get is information with no practical application. And 2 Corinthians 3:6 puts it like this: "The letter killeth, but the spirit makes it alive." Just doing research and providing historical and theological information does not bring life. It is when you allow the spirit of God to transform that information into practical application that it brings life to the hearers.

So, all information with no practical application is a dull sermon. All practical application with no theological information is a watered down and, more than likely, incorrect sermon.

With this method, each question has a purpose. You need all three of the purposes in order to fully get the impact of the method. However, the answers are subject to the preacher in terms of quantity. Maybe you can answer each question in one answer. There are some questions I've answered in two answers, while answering another question in one answer and answering another question in three answers. It is contextual to the preacher, and it gives the flexibility for the preacher to be themselves at whatever juncture of the sermon that they're at based on the answers they choose. Remember: You make the questions; you choose the answers. By the grace of God, your meditation moments, your prayer time, and your study, you understand what you want to convey to the hearers. So, you cut the cloth to fit the garment in terms of how many answers you give. But you need the three questions in order for the whole method to be complete.

Step 1: Research

The context to make the sermon and the Three-Question Method better is based on the process of construction. So, the process of composition for this method is research, narrative, practical application, and development of the questions and answers in that order. Before you come up with any questions or answers, you must first do research. The Three-Question Method is most effective when you've learned everything you can possibly learn about that pericope, that particular biblical story, or even that particular book of the bible to which you are referencing. The more you learn, the more impactful this method is. So, research is key. You have to learn everything you can about the text that you are focusing on. What is the current culture of the people in the text? Who are we talking about? What is the history of the city, nation, ethnicity of the particular persons who you are about to preach about? Even if you do not use all of this information within the sermon, it will help you to articulate with conviction the parts that you will use while preaching. As preachers, it is our job to be the educator within that moment without boring the people with mere information.

How you research is based on the individual preacher. Some are visual learners; some are auditory learners; some are avid readers; some read through hearing the book in audio books. The key is to get the research in before you do anything else, whether it's constructing the thesis statement, coming up with the questions or the answers, or making the moves and the turns in the sermon. After praying, before you do anything else, you're going to do your research. 2 Timothy 2:15 is clear that we should "study to show thyself approved to God, a workman that needeth not be ashamed rightly dividing the word of truth." I cannot emphasize this enough... study, study, study.

Once you've done your research, then you can move to the narrative. You have to find the life in the theme that the research is throwing at you. Remember: You and the Holy Spirit are the only two people in the room after you've gone through all of the information your research has provided. That's when the Lord can speak to you. And now, you have your narrative. Your narrative is the argument of the story that you are about to tell or the picture that you're about to paint in the minds of people through a sermonic presentation. Once you have your narrative, then you can understand the practical application that the narrative is supposed to bring out in a general sense.

In other words, what is now the central theme that you see in all of the information that you have researched? What position are you coming from, based on your research, that you feel is the bottom-line message of this sermon? You may have had one thought in mind before the research. After you have studied, however, what is in your heart now that lines up with the accuracy of your research? Now that you have all of the information, you can make an informed presentation of conveying the Gospel.

Be okay with your thought process changing once you have done your homework. Nothing messes up a great idea for a sermon like research does. This deviation from your original idea is totally acceptable because now, you can rightly divide the Word since you have studied. Your entire sermon may shift the more you study and research. That shift is what information does. Your job is to make sure you find the practical application, even within the shifting of the sermon.

Once you have the practical application in your head, you're ready to develop the questions and the answers. Until then, until you have done the research, built a narrative, and understood the practical application of the narrative based on the research, you're not ready for questions and answers. Up until the point of understanding, you don't even know what questions to ask.

There is a reason that the introduction "sermon in a sentence" stands on its own apart from the question. The reason it's not an additional question is because, as stated earlier, that "sermon in a sentence" is the central theme of the sermon. You know that the questions and answers are accurate, and that the sermon is in synergy based on the fact that the questions and answers all revolve around the central theme. So, it's not that it stands alone in the sermon—that "sermon in a sentence" is the *center* of the sermon. All questions and answers should revolve around and tie back to that "sermon in a sentence" by the time of practical application.

Step 2: Question 1 — What is the context?

This first question is based on the backdrop of the text. If you are going to prove the point of the central theme throughout the sermon, then you must first give context, also known as background information. Bring the hearers up to speed on what is going on in the background of the text. If the text is an epistle, a psalm, a stanza, a proverb, etc., then give the people a backstory. Who is writing it? Who are they writing to? What is the situation during the time of the text? What person, or group of people, is involved in the text?

Again, allow me to use the *Humpty Dumpty* example. Again, I use this illustration in order to break down the steps in the simplest form to give understanding to the method. The first question can be related to the main character: Who is this text dealing with? The answer could be as simple as saying, "An individual who made a slippery decision." At this point, a narrative is required to bring the hearer up to speed regarding what is happening to bring us to this text. Humpty Dumpty, this individual of obvious nobility, decided to sit where he could see everything, but he could not maintain his posture.

You close out the first point by giving the practical application of telling the hearers what that particular information has to do with their lives in today's context. Maybe talk about how actions have consequences, even if those consequences were unintentional. Follow that practical application up with real-life examples. There must always be a moment at the end of the narrative that ties that particular context into what that information has to do with everyday life. Giving the practical application will help you open the door to the second question.

For example, using the Humpty Dumpty narrative, the practical application in this moment could speak to the fact that you must always be conscious of whether or not the environment to which you have placed yourself in can handle the weight of who you are. Unlike Humpty, we must be realistic in our assessment and expectation that the places we have chosen to hang out in can handle who we are made to be. This conveyed humanistic truth, if this were a Biblical text, is considered a practical application. This practical application is how you would end the first question and open the door to transition into the second question.

Step 3: Question 2 — Where is the tension in the text?

This question is where we expose the not-so-pretty side of the truth within the text. These are the questions that you would ask that best friend who didn't necessarily make the right choices, but who you are close enough with to hold them accountable. In your research, it is totally proper to ask the hard questions. Confronting people where they are has always been the assignment of prophets in biblical times. What makes the job of today's preaching prophets any different?

Pick a hard question. If Humpty Dumpty were a real biblical character, it would be okay in this sense to ask questions such as: "What possessed you to try that?" "Why would you sit THERE?" "Who convinced you that this was a good idea, and why would you listen to them?" This line of questioning reveals the tension, or the hard truth, of the situation. Since we can see the relevancy of questioning a fictional character such as Humpty Dumpty, then how much more relevant would it be for us to ask those kinds of questions of people like King David, Moses, Apostle Paul, the twelve disciples with Jesus, and even Jesus himself? This second question requires that tension. Ask the hard questions so as to bring the sermon right where the people listening are.

Your research will help you to answer the question. You have done your homework, so you know parts about the story that most people wouldn't. Use that information to answer the question. If Humpty were a real-life character, then maybe we could ask, "Why would Humpty Dumpty sit on a wall that wasn't built for him?" At this point, the answer should challenge the hearer to look at their own lives. The answer could be as simple as him trying to do what was not designed for him while trying to be like everybody else that he saw. Again, the answer to the question should end with a shift to practical application. Remind the hearers at this point what this has to do with our lives today. Ending this narrative with practical application is the transition into the third question.

Step 4: Question 3 — What is the resolution of the text?

By the time we get to the third question, the hearers should have the picture painted of the central theme. The sermon in a sentence has come to life without you reiterating it over and over again. The hearers should be able to relate because the preacher has made the text come to life right in front of their faces. There should be a metaphorical mirror that has been held up to the audience, and they should feel as if this bible really does relate to their everyday lives. This revelation of relativity is what sets up the sermon for the third question.

The third question is the prognosis, or the prescription, of the text. The question is slightly easier to come by because it should include the title of the sermon. If the title cannot, in any way, tie into the third question, then the solution to that challenge is simple: Change the title. Similar to the application method, the preacher must ask an empowering question that requires an empowering answer.

This answer does not mean that it will necessarily be what the listener wants to hear. The answer does, however, empower behavioral modification. The answer could also encourage the people paying attention to stay on the right path. Whatever the answer is, the importance is that it comes out of the text. If, in fact, the answer is not found in the text, it is not a good answer for this particular method. This answer that is not in the text may provoke another question for the preacher: Do you have the right text? The answers must be found in the text in some way, shape, or form.

The beauty of the third question is that the preacher gets to decide how many answers are given based on how many things the preacher sees in the text. For the sake of brevity, I will just give the example of maybe one answer in our fictional text. Maybe the title could be something like "Fixing Irreparable Brokenness." So, the question would be something to the manner of, "How is this brokenness irreparable"? If we were to pull an answer out of this fictional text, perhaps it would be something about the situation being left in the wrong hands—the king's horses and the king's men.

The third question's answer, or answers, should provoke action on the part of the hearer. The answer should make sense to the hearers' everyday lives. The resolution, however, must come from the text. If the preacher has done their homework, this part of the sermon preparation should be the most exciting part. You have used the first two questions to build up to the point of the third question: truly trying to help people live better lives. Helping people at this point should provoke a moment of celebration within the close.

Step 5: Celebrating/Closing the Sermon

Regardless of where the last question's answer lands, the preacher should find a point to give hope to the people listening. Even if the sermon does require hard work in the resolution, at least find hope to convey that it is possible, based on who we hold on to, to make it possible. Once that hope is found in the text, then the preacher can close the sermon on a note of encouragement, empowerment, and enlightenment.

This enlightenment is what makes all of the previous components worth the journey for both the preacher and the hearer. The preacher feels that they have confidently conveyed what they believe God has placed on their hearts, and the people have an understanding of a portion of the bible that will stick with them long after the sermon is preached.

The closing of the sermon is the shortest part. That brief moment of celebration is what brings validation to the rest of the lesson. The defining moment as to the synergy of the sermon is when, at the end of the close, the "sermon in a sentence" from the beginning of the sermon can be quoted again at the end of the sermon, and it all makes sense to the hearers. That defining moment is when the preacher should know, regardless of them having a different style of delivery than everyone else, that they have properly handled their assignment.

CONCLUSION

Power Back to the Pews: God puts ownership of delivering the message to the preacher. It is the preacher's job to give ownership of applying the message to the people. It is then the responsibility of the people to apply that message to their lives. Romans 10:14 says, "How, then, shall they call on him in whom they have not believed? And how shall they believe in him whom they have not heard? And how shall they hear without a preacher?" The power of the message comes from God and is given to the preacher. That power given to the preacher should be then given to the pews to apply that same power in their own individual contexts. This constant transfer of ownership and power only happens when there is effective preaching. Effective preaching can be intentional, concise, authentic, and relevant, while still conscious of time management, in order to impact the hearer. This, my friend, depicts the mentality of preaching via the Three-Question Method.

There is importance in knowing that preaching is not just mechanics. Preaching is a mentality. Whether it's the mentality of attaching preaching to church revitalization or simply being an itinerant preacher, preaching is more than mechanics. How the preacher sees things in the text when they study, is able to see life in a worldview that helps them to challenge a diverse audience, and can use everyday life moments to synergize the theological with the practical doesn't just speak to the preacher's ability; these moves are a developed mentality. This Three-Question Method requires more than just a gift; it requires devotion to development. This development is spiritual, theological, and in conjunction with a mentality to constantly grow and properly help God's people.

Acknowledgments

I would like to take this time to acknowledge people who are influential to me in ministry. First, my pastor, Dr. Lewis N. Watson. Thank you for exposing me to levels of ministry that I had only seen from an extreme distance. You opened my eyes to the potential impact in ministry that my life carried, and I am grateful.

Second, I would like to acknowledge my spiritual covering, Bishop Anthony G. Maclin. Your support, encouragement, and guidance during some rough seasons of my life have been invaluable to me and my ministry. I am forever grateful for you, your life, and your ministry.

Third, I would like to acknowledge the Christian Unity Baptist Church. Thank you for allowing me to be me, and for the opportunity for us to do ministry together. It is because of your love and support that I have not been limited in my ability to operate in any gifts that God has given me. I love you all, and there is NOTHING that you can do about it!

ABOUT THE AUTHOR

Rev. Dr. Antione J. Hutchins, D.Ed.Min. serves as Senior Pastor of the Christian Unity Baptist Church of Waldorf, Maryland. The church has grown from a handful to many hundreds in a short period of time. His passions include preaching, teaching, church revitalization, and church administration.

Dr. Hutchins earned a Bachelor of Theology degree from the National School of Theology. He holds a Master of Divinity degree from the Virginia Union University Samuel DeWitt Proctor School of Theology. Dr. Hutchins earned a Doctor of Educational Ministry degree from the Boyce College Southern Baptist Theological Seminary in Louisville, Kentucky.

Dr. Hutchins is the President and CEO of AJH Church Administration Consulting, also known as CAC. CAC is a ministry that provides church staff training, clergy contract mediation, and senior pastor consultant support.

In addition to being an itinerant national evangelist, Dr. Hutchins facilitates an annual program of preaching mentorship affectionately called "Preaching Bootcamp," preparing generations of preachers to operate in their calling of proclaiming the Gospel.

Dr. Hutchins is on a mandate by God to teach the people of God the value of worship, while bringing the revelation of God's Word in a practical way, so that people may grasp and apply it to everyday life.

Contact Info:

Website: www.ajhutchins.com

Email: Ajhutchins2.0@gmail.com

Facebook: @ajhutchins2.0

Instagram: @ajhutchins2.0

Twitter: @ajhutchins